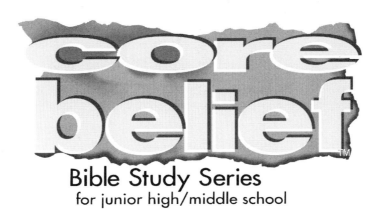

Bible Study Series
for junior high/middle school

THE TRUTH ABOUT Worship

Loveland, Colorado

The Truth About Worship
Core Belief Bible Study Series
Copyright © 1998 Group Publishing, Inc.

All rights reserved. No part of this book may be reproduced in any manner whatsoever without prior written permission from the publisher, except where noted in the text and in the case of brief quotations embodied in critical articles and reviews. For information, write Permissions, Group Publishing, Inc., Dept. PD, P.O. Box 481, Loveland, CO 80539.

Credits
Editor: Karl Leuthauser
Creative Development Editors: Ivy Beckwith and Paul Woods
Chief Creative Officer: Joani Schultz
Copy Editor: Candace McMahan
Art Director: Ray Tollison
Cover Art Director: Jeff A. Storm
Computer Graphic Artist/Illustrator: Eris Klein
Photographer: FPG International
Production Manager: Gingar Kunkel

Unless otherwise noted, Scriptures quoted from the HOLY BIBLE, NEW INTERNATIONAL VERSION®. Copyright © 1973, 1978, 1984 by International Bible Society. Used by permission of Zondervan Publishing House. All rights reserved.

ISBN 0-7644-0867-4

10 9 8 7 6 5 4 3 2 1   07 06 05 04 03 02 01 00 99 98

Printed in the United States of America.

contents:

the Core Belief: Worship

Worship isn't a foreign concept to young people. They often devote themselves to celebrities of all sorts. Yet celebrities will inevitably disappoint them as the celebrities fade away or fall.

But God never fails. He is worthy of our worship. He always does what he says; he never does anything wrong; and when we give him our worship, he draws us closer in a loving embrace.

Through this book, kids can discover that worship is an essential aspect of following God. They'll also explore how worship has both individual and corporate components. Personal worship involves times of expressing praise and gratitude to God, but it should also permeate our lifestyles as we express our praise and serve God through all we do. Corporate worship entails gathering with other believers and together responding to all God is and all he's done.

Worship is a vital element of our Christianity. Not only is God pleased by our worship, he also uses it to refresh us spiritually and renew our lives' focus.

the Helpful Stuff

WORSHIP AS A CORE CHRISTIAN BELIEF — **7**
(or Giving Credit Where It's Due)

ABOUT CORE BELIEF BIBLE STUDY SERIES — **10**
(or How to Move Mountains in One Hour or Less)

WHY ACTIVE AND INTERACTIVE LEARNING WORKS WITH TEENAGERS — **57**
(or How to Keep Your Kids Awake)

YOUR EVALUATION — **63**
(or How You Can Edit Our Stuff Without Getting Paid)

the ▼ Studies

Teen Idols 15
THE ISSUE: Idolatry
THE BIBLE CONNECTION: Exodus 20:3-6; 32:1-8; and Matthew 4:8-10
THE POINT: We're created with the need to worship.

24-Hour Worship 25
THE ISSUE: Worship
THE BIBLE CONNECTION: Various passages from 1 Samuel; 2 Samuel; and Psalms
THE POINT: You can worship God in everything you do.

Stress Reliever 35
THE ISSUE: Stress
THE BIBLE CONNECTION: Exodus 18:13-26; Ruth 1:3-18; Nehemiah 4:1-9; 6:1-9; Matthew 6:25-34; 11:28-30; Acts 15:36-41; and Romans 12:1-2
THE POINT: Worship helps you focus on what's important.

A New Song, a True Song 45
THE ISSUE: Authenticity
THE BIBLE CONNECTION: Psalms 103:1-18; 113:1-9; John 4:23-24; Romans 8:31-39; and Ephesians 2:13-22
THE POINT: Worship is a true celebration.

Worship as a Core Christian Belief

Kids know about worship. They worship musicians, movie stars, professional athletes, and possessions. Kids put posters on their walls, T-shirts on their bodies, headsets over their ears, and even tattoos on their skin—all to exalt human beings and material products.

Unfortunately the "little gods" kids find to praise and honor often disappoint them. The objects of worship become old, out-of-date, or just plain boring.

Thankfully, there's an alternative. God goes beyond fads, marketing, and fame. Worshiping the Creator is exciting, enduring, and fulfilling because God is the only one worthy of our praise and adoration.

This study course will help your kids understand what true and worthwhile worship is all about. First, they'll talk about the little gods in their lives as they examine modern **idolatry**. Through their investigation, kids can discover that they're created with a need to worship and that if they aren't worshiping God, they're worshiping someone or something else.

In the second study, they'll focus on ways they can **worship** through their daily activities. They'll discover that God is just as real and available to them at home, in school, or anywhere else as he is when they are in church.

The third study will help kids see that worship helps us focus on what's important. They'll be encouraged to look to God in an attitude of worship when their lives are chaotic and difficult and when they are feeling overwhelmed by **stress**.

The final study will challenge kids to take an honest look at how they worship. They'll have the opportunity to discover that God isn't interested in coerced praise. God desires praise that is motivated by **authenticity**—praise that comes from understanding who God is and what he does.

God is worthy of kids' worship. And they need to understand that worship is more than mindlessly singing a couple of hymns or choruses. When kids realize that God wants worship to permeate all they do and they begin to practice true worship, they'll bring honor to God and spiritual enrichment to their lives.

For a more comprehensive look at this Core Christian Belief, read Group's ***Get Real: Making Core Christian Beliefs Relevant to Teenagers.***

DEPTH FINDER
HOW THE BIBLE DESCRIBES WORSHIP

To help you effectively guide your kids toward this Core Christian Belief, use these overviews as a launching point for a more in-depth study of worship.

- **Worship is essential to following God.** The Hebrew word translated "worship" literally means to "bow down." It refers to the honor and reverence shown to a superior being. God is the only one worthy of such worship. In a sense, God both initiates and receives our worship, since the Holy Spirit working in us prompts us to worship God. Through our worship, we express our adoration to God and draw closer to him as we ascribe to him the honor due only to God. We worship God because of who he is, acknowledging his awesomeness and admitting our own smallness.

  Worship can be offered through words, music, giving, silent prayers, and many other forms. Worship includes obedience and service; words of praise coming from the mouth of a disobedient Christian mean little to God. We also worship God when we demonstrate a faith commitment through baptism and when we remember Jesus' sacrifice by celebrating the Lord's Supper (Psalms 24:3-4; 27:8; 29:2; 96:8; Isaiah 6:3; Matthew 4:10; Luke 6:46; John 6:44; Acts 10:46-48; 1 Corinthians 11:23-26; 1 Peter 2:5; Revelation 15:4).

- **Worship should be individual.** Though the Bible describes worship primarily as something the faithful do together, personal worship is an essential part of the Christian's life. The Psalmist worshiped God wherever he was and, many times, by himself. Worshiping together with other Christians at church does not take the place of individual times of solitary prayer and praise. Personal worship involves times of orally or silently expressing our praise and gratitude to God. But worship is also a lifestyle; part of worshiping God is caring about and helping people who are hurting (2 Samuel 22:4; Psalms 28:7; 34:1; Isaiah 58:6-11; Micah 6:8; Matthew 5:16; 14:22-23; Romans 12:1).

- **Worship should be corporate.** In both the Old and New Testaments, worship most often appears in the context of God's people gathering together to offer him praise. In worship, the church responds together to who God is and what he has done for us. Corporate worship generally involves active, focused participation by all the members of the local church. Whether people within a congregation are singing, giving offerings, praying, dancing, or offering silent or oral praises, the only people really worshiping are those who are genuinely focusing on God. When we focus on God in worship, we not only please our creator, we receive spiritual refreshing and focus in our lives (Psalms 95:6; 96:1-9; Luke 19:37; 1 Peter 2:9-10; 1 John 1:3).

CORE CHRISTIAN BELIEF OVERVIEW

Here are the twenty-four Core Christian Belief categories that form the backbone of Core Belief Bible Study Series:

The Nature of God	Jesus Christ	The Holy Spirit
Humanity	Evil	Suffering
Creation	The Spiritual Realm	The Bible
Salvation	Spiritual Growth	Personal Character
God's Justice	Sin & Forgiveness	The Last Days
Love	The Church	Worship
Authority	Prayer	Family
Service	Relationships	Sharing Faith

Look for Group's Core Belief Bible Study Series books in these other Core Christian Beliefs!

about

Bible Study Series
for junior high/middle school

Think for a moment about your young people. When your students walk out of your youth program after they graduate from junior high or high school, what do you want them to know? What foundation do you want them to have so they can make wise choices?

You probably want them to know the essentials of the Christian faith. You want them to base everything they do on the foundational truths of Christianity. Are you meeting this goal?

If you have any doubt that your kids will walk into adulthood knowing and living by the tenets of the Christian faith, then you've picked up the right book. All the books in Group's Core Belief Bible Study Series encourage young people to discover the essentials of Christianity and to put those essentials into practice. Let us explain...

What Is Group's Core Belief Bible Study Series?

Group's Core Belief Bible Study Series is a biblically in-depth study series for junior high and senior high teenagers. This Bible study series utilizes four defining commitments to create each study. These "plumb lines" provide structure and continuity for every activity, study, project, and discussion. They are:

● **A Commitment to Biblical Depth**—Core Belief Bible Study Series is founded on the belief that kids not only *can* understand the deeper truths of the Bible but also *want* to understand them. Therefore, the activities and studies in this series strive to explain the "why" behind every truth we explore. That way, kids learn principles, not just rules.

● **A Commitment to Relevance**—Most kids aren't interested in abstract theories or doctrines about the universe. They want to know how to live successfully right now, today, in the heat of problems they can't ignore. Because of this, each study connects a real-life need with biblical principles that speak directly to that need. This study series finally bridges the gap between Bible truths and the real-world issues kids face.

● **A Commitment to Variety**—Today's young people have been raised in a sound bite world. They demand variety. For that reason, no two meetings in this study series are shaped exactly the same.

● **A Commitment to Active and Interactive Learning**—Active learning is learning by doing. Interactive learning simply takes active learning a step further by having kids teach each other what they've learned. It's a process that helps kids internalize and remember their discoveries.

For a more detailed description of these concepts, see the section titled "Why Active and Interactive Learning Works With Teenagers" beginning on page 57.

So how can you accomplish all this in a set of four easy-to-lead Bible studies? By weaving together various "power" elements to produce a fun experience that leaves kids challenged and encouraged.

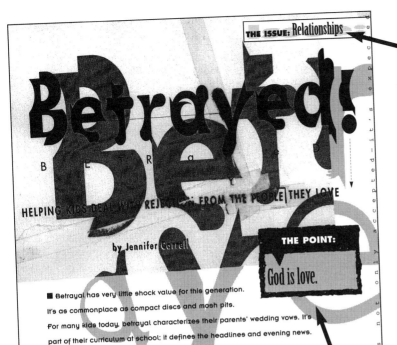

- **A Relevant Topic**—More than ever before, kids live in the now. What matters to them and what attracts their hearts is what's happening in their world at this moment. For this reason, every Core Belief Bible Study focuses on a particular hot topic that kids care about.

- **A Core Christian Belief**—Group's Core Belief Bible Study Series organizes the wealth of Christian truth and experience into twenty-four Core Christian Belief categories. These twenty-four headings act as umbrellas for a collection of detailed beliefs that define Christianity and set it apart from the world and every other religion. Each book in this series features one Core Christian Belief with lessons suited for junior high or senior high students.

  "But," you ask, "won't my kids be bored talking about all these spiritual beliefs?" No way! As a youth leader, you know the value of using hot topics to connect with young people. Ultimately teenagers talk about issues because they're searching for meaning in their lives. They want to find the one equation that will make sense of all the confusing events happening around them. Each Core Belief Bible Study answers that need by connecting a hot topic with a powerful Christian principle. Kids walk away from the study with something more solid than just the shifting ebb and flow of their own opinions. They walk away with a deeper understanding of their Christian faith.

- **The Point**—This simple statement is designed to be the intersection between the Core Christian Belief and the hot topic. Everything in the study ultimately focuses on The Point so that kids study it and allow it time to sink into their hearts.

- **The Study at a Glance**—A quick look at this chart will tell you what kids will do, how long it will take them to do it, and what supplies you'll need to get it done.

Helpful Stuff   11

- **The Bible Connection**—This is the power base of each study. Whether it's just one verse or several chapters, The Bible Connection provides the vital link between kids' minds and their hearts. The content of each Core Belief Bible Study reflects the belief that the true power of God—the power to expose, heal, and change kids' lives—is contained in his Word.

- **Depthfinder Boxes**—These informative sidelights located throughout each study add insight into a particular passage, word, historical fact, or Christian doctrine. Depthfinder boxes also provide insight into teen culture, adolescent development, current events, and philosophy.

- **Leader Tips**—These handy information boxes coach you through the study, offering helpful suggestions on everything from altering activities for different-sized groups to streamlining discussions to using effective discipline techniques.

- **Handouts**—Most Core Belief Bible Studies include photocopiable handouts to use with your group. Handouts might take the form of a fun game, a lively discussion starter, or a challenging study page for kids to take home—anything to make your study more meaningful and effective.

Helpful Stuff 12

The Last Word on Core Belief Bible Studies

Soon after you begin to use Group's Core Belief Bible Study Series, you'll see signs of real growth in your group members. Your kids will gain a deeper understanding of the Bible and of their own Christian faith. They'll see more clearly how a relationship with Jesus affects their daily lives. And they'll grow closer to God.

But that's not all. You'll also see kids grow closer to one another.

That's because this series is founded on the principle that Christian faith grows best in the context of relationship. Each study uses a variety of interactive pairs and small groups and always includes discussion questions that promote deeper relationships. The friendships kids will build through this study series will enable them to grow *together* toward a deeper relationship with God.

THE ISSUE: Idolatry

teen idols

Focusing Kids' Worship on God

by Cindy S. Hansen

■ According to William Mahedy and Janet Bernardi, authors of A Generation Alone, each of us has a "God space"—a space within us that only God can fill. Mahedy and Bernardi describe this space: "This shape is the same for every person and is present in a very clear form from birth. It is...so large that many people cannot define it or see it is there." ■ We're created to adore and serve God. But being sinful people, we often misdirect our worship. We try to fill our God space with money, relationships, belongings, and achievements. Your young people might try to fill this space with clothes, friends, grades, adrenalin rushes, or computer-generated experiences. ■ But these kinds of attempts to fill the God space don't work. Mahedy and Bernardi say, "Trying to fill the God space with such things is like tossing goldfish into the mouth of a whale." ■ We can only fill that space when we worship the one true God. ■ This study introduces your young people to their need to worship and challenges them to fill this need by worshiping God above all else.

THE POINT:

> We're created with the need to worship.

The Study
AT A GLANCE

SECTION	MINUTES	WHAT STUDENTS WILL DO	SUPPLIES
Introducing Idolatry	5 to 10	MOST VALUABLE—"Vote" for what they deem most valuable in their lives.	Slips of paper, pencils, tape, newsprint, marker
Bible Investigation	10 to 15	QUOTES TO NOTE—Discuss quotes and Scriptures about idolatry and worship.	Bibles
Reflection	20 to 25	IS IT AN IDOL?—Demonstrate how common interests can become idols.	Paper, pens
	5 to 10	OFF BALANCE—Pray while balancing on one foot then while standing on both feet.	

notes:

THE POINT OF "TEEN IDOLS":

We're created with the need to worship.

THE BIBLE CONNECTION

EXODUS 20:3-6	God commands his people to worship only him.
EXODUS 32:1-8	Aaron makes a golden calf for the Israelites to worship.
MATTHEW 4:8-10	Satan tempts Jesus to worship him, and Jesus resists.

In this study, kids will vote on the most valuable things in their lives, discuss quotes and Scriptures on worship, and demonstrate how common interests can become objects of worship.

Through this experience, kids can discover their inborn need to worship and will learn that they can only fulfill this need when they worship the one true God.

Explore the verses in The Bible Connection, then examine the information in the Depthfinder boxes throughout the study to gain a deeper understanding of how these Scriptures connect with your young people.

THE STUDY

LEADER TIP for The Study

Because this topic can be so powerful and relevant to kids' lives, your group members may be tempted to get caught up in issues and lose sight of the deeper biblical principle found in The Point. Help your kids grasp The Point by guiding them to focus on the biblical investigation and discussing how God's truth connects with reality in their lives.

INTRODUCING IDOLATRY ▼

Most Valuable (5 to 10 minutes) As kids arrive, give each one a slip of paper and a pencil. Say: **We're going to take a "most valuable" vote. Write down something you deem the most valuable thing in your life, such as a person, sport, pet, hobby, or possession.**

When kids have finished, have each student read his or her "vote" to the class. On a sheet of newsprint taped to a wall, record

Teen Idols   17

LEADER TIP for The Study

Whenever you ask pairs or other groups to discuss a list of questions, write the questions on newsprint, and tape the newsprint to a wall so groups can answer the questions at their own pace.

each student's vote. If a student repeats another student's item, place a tally mark after that item. When all the students have read their votes, count the tally marks to see which item was voted most valuable by the class. Then have kids form foursomes to discuss these questions:

- **How did you choose what to vote for?**
- **How has your "most valuable" item affected your life?**
- **Has the item you chose ever disappointed you? Explain.**
- **What does it mean to worship something?**
- **Do you worship the item you said was the most valuable? Explain.**

Say: <u>We're created with the need to worship.</u> We can determine what we worship by thinking about what we place above everything else. Today we're going to explore how God wants us to worship him, making him number one in our lives.

BIBLE INVESTIGATION ▼

Quotes to Note (10 to 15 minutes) Have kids form groups of four. Say: **I'd like you to listen to the following quotation by Charles Barkley. Then discuss a few questions within your group.** Read the following quotation aloud:

"I don't understand why people would buy one sneaker endorsed by one player over the other. Kids idolize professional athletes, which is wrong in itself, and they just copy what they're wearing...To kids that idolize me, I tell them don't do so just because I can dribble a basketball—that's really sick."

—Charles Barkley, professional basketball player (quoted in *The Performance Illusion* by Chap Clark)

DEPTHFINDER — UNDERSTANDING WORSHIP

We can worship God in two ways. First, we can worship God by expressing our love and adoration for him (see Isaiah 12:4-6). Through prayer and singing, we can express everything we appreciate about God and can declare our ultimate devotion to him. Second, we can worship God by serving him (see Matthew 4:10). When we realize how great God is and how much he's given us, we often want to respond by giving our time, energy, and money back to him. *The Disciple's Study Bible* explains the intertwining of these two ways of worshiping God: "True worship involves a willingness to serve, and genuine service to God must be accompanied by a sense of reverence and adoration."

To remember these two aspects of worship, visualize the cross. The vertical piece represents the adoration and reverence we lift up to God. The horizontal piece represents our reaching out to others through service. (See handout on page 23.) Together, they form a complete picture of worship—our response to God for the sacrifice he made on our behalf.

Teen Idols 18

DEPTHFINDER: UNDERSTANDING THE BIBLE

In the Old Testament, God's chosen people, the Israelites, lived among cultures that created and worshiped idols. Exposure to these practices often influenced the Israelites to worship idols, too, directly opposing God's commandments against worshiping anyone or anything other than him (see Exodus 20:3-6).

The Zondervan Pictorial Encyclopedia of the Bible (vol. H–L, p. 248) explains why idolatry is vehemently forbidden: "Idolatry is vigorously condemned both in the [Old Testament] and [New Testament] because it degrades both God and man. It denies the existence of the true God who created the world and mankind, and whose glory cannot be adequately captured in any tangible form. It is absurd that a person could carve an idol with his own hands and then be afraid of what he has made."

However, like the Israelites in the wilderness worshiping the golden calf, we often find it easier to idolize what we can tangibly experience. Created with the need to worship, we devote ourselves to our own creations, whether they be relationships, achievements, or possessions.

Moses spent forty days on the mountain with God. While he was away, the Israelites began to doubt. They probably were frightened that he wouldn't return and that his mysterious God left with him. Like the Israelites, we sometimes doubt when we can't see or hear God's work in our lives.

But our inability to perceive him tangibly doesn't diminish his ability to care for us. Our Creator is worthy of our singular devotion, and we can only truly fulfill our need to worship when we place God first in our lives.

Have groups discuss:
- **Do you agree with Charles Barkley? Why or why not?**
- **Why do you think some people idolize professional athletes?**
- **Do you think the admiration people have for sports figures is the same thing as worship? Why or why not?**
- **Read Exodus 32:1-8. What are some modern false gods?**
- **Do you have any false gods in your life? If so, what are they?**
- **Read Matthew 4:8-10. How does God feel about false gods?**

After kids finish their discussions, have them discuss the following quotation by Annie Dillard:

"Worship is dangerous. It is not a retreat from reality, but a direct engagement with ultimate reality: God. Genuine worship is a response to God and what he has done; in it we make ourselves vulnerable to the story of Israel and Jesus. Does anyone have the foggiest idea what sort of power we so blithely invoke? The churches are children playing on the floor with their chemistry sets, mixing up a batch of TNT to kill a Sunday morning. It is madness to wear ladies' straw hats and velvet hats to church; we should all be wearing crash helmets. Ushers should issue life preservers and signal flares; they should lash us to our pews."

—Annie Dillard (quoted in *People of the Truth*, excerpted by Chap Clark in *The Performance Illusion*)

Have groups discuss:
- **Do you agree with Annie Dillard's understanding of worship?**

Why or why not?

- How is her description like your worship experiences? How is it different?
- Read Exodus 20:3-6. What hazards are involved in worshiping false gods?
- What blessings are involved in worshiping God?

After kids finish discussing the questions, have the group come together. Ask:

- **Do you think <u>we're created with the need to worship</u>?**
- **What is the purpose of worship?**
- Why do you think God wants us to focus on him and not on other things or people?
- How can you make God the number one focus in your life?

Say: **The Israelites disobeyed God by giving in to the temptation to worship an idol. Jesus was also tempted to worship someone other than God, but he responded differently. In your groups, read aloud Matthew 4:8-10.**

After groups have read the passage, have them discuss these questions:

- How did Jesus respond to Satan's temptation to worship him?
- What might have happened if Jesus had chosen to worship Satan instead of God?
- How might Satan tempt us to worship him or other things instead of God? Why would he do this?
- What can we learn from Jesus about resisting the temptation to place something or someone else above God?
- What are some strategies we can use to resist the temptation to idolize people or things?

"You shall have no other gods before me. You shall not make for yourself an idol in the form of anything

in heaven above

or on the earth beneath

or in the waters below."

Exodus 20:3-4

After a few minutes, invite groups to share their insights from the discussion. Then say: **Satan tempted Jesus to worship him. But Jesus resisted that temptation by reciting Scripture about worshiping only God. We're created with the need to worship, and we face temptation to fill this need by placing friends, relatives, school, sports, and other things first in our lives. But we can only fill this need completely when we choose to worship God above everything else.**

If you don't have a relationship with Jesus Christ, you may not know what it means to worship God. If you'd like to know more, I'd love to talk with you after class.

REFLECTION ▼

Is It an Idol? (20 to 25 minutes) Say: **We know that God wants us to have fun, but God also want us to keep him above everything else in our lives.** Ask:

● **What's the difference between worshiping something and enjoying something?**

Have kids form groups of four. Assign one of the following interests to each group:
- friends
- television
- sports
- reading
- music
- computers
- boyfriends/girlfriends
- popularity

Say: **With your group, I'd like you to develop a short skit that demonstrates the difference between enjoyment and idolatry. Through your skits, show how your interest could become an idol. For example, if your interest is sports, your group could create a skit that shows an athlete who's sacrificed everything, including his or her relationship with God, for the sport.**

Give kids about five minutes to prepare, then have each group present its skit. After each skit ask:

● **How can this interest be an idol?**
● **How can this interest be a positive thing?**
● **How can you make sure this interest doesn't become an idol in your life?**

After all the skits have been discussed, ask:

● **What are some others things that serve as idols in the lives of teenagers?**
● **How do you fill your need to worship?**
● **Is it possible to worship God through some of the interests we've talked about? Explain.**

Give each student a sheet of paper and a pen. Ask teenagers to list

LEADER TIP for Is It an Idol?

Consider providing props for the skits. For example, you could include hats, coats, cardboard boxes, athletic equipment, and a telephone. Encourage kids to be creative with the props.

all the things in their lives that serve as idols. Tell kids to take three minutes to ask God to show them which idols need to be dealt with immediately and how they should be dealt with.

After three minutes of silence, give kids an opportunity to share what they discovered about the idols in their lives. Say: **We're created with the need to worship. It's possible to worship God in the things we enjoy, but it's also possible to make those things the objects of our worship. Sometimes we need to give those things up, but sometimes we just need to readjust our focus by concentrating on the real reasons for doing what we do.**

Off Balance (5 to 10 minutes)

Say: **Now let's ask God to help us place him above everything else.** Tell kids to balance on one foot as you begin the prayer. Ask kids to refrain from leaning on others. Pray: **Dear God, please hear us as we confess those things we place ahead of you in our lives.** As kids continue to balance, invite them to pray silently about things they place ahead of God in their lives. Pray: **When we place anything ahead of you, our lives are out of balance. We're created with the need to worship. Please show us how to fill this need by worshiping you.**

Direct kids to place both feet firmly on the ground, then pray: **Help us remember to keep you first in our lives. We'll stand on solid ground when we do.** Instruct kids to praise God for who he is and what he has done. When all your students have had an opportunity to pray, say: **Amen.**

THE ISSUE: Worship

24-Hour WORSHIP

Worshiping God in Everything We Do

by Lisa Baba Lauffer

■ What do skateboarding, playing the guitar, writing a composition, hanging out at youth group, washing dishes, talking to a friend, eating ice cream straight from the carton, and delivering papers have in common? They're all opportunities to worship God! ■ The idea of worship can seem stale and dull to your young people. Many teenagers associate worship with a stark sanctuary, boring sermons, and ancient music. And that's a shame. Because worship in its truest sense is more colorful, alive, and dynamic than anything your kids usually associate with worship. How could it be any different when it's the result of contact with our living, holy, creative, merciful, almighty God? ■ And your students can worship God at any moment of any day. ■ This study invites your students to view worship in a new way—as a continuous response to a growing, vital relationship with God.

THE POINT:

You can worship God in everything you do.

The Study
AT A GLANCE

SECTION	MINUTES	WHAT STUDENTS WILL DO	SUPPLIES
Time Line Creation	10 to 15	A DAY IN THE LIFE—Create time lines indicating what they did the day before the study.	Masking tape, pens, paper, tape, newsprint, markers
Interactive Bible Experience	25 to 35	ENCOUNTERS WITH GOD—Explore events in David's life and his worshipful responses to those events and compare David's responses to their own in similar circumstances.	Bibles, "David's Daily Worship" handouts (p. 33), refreshments
Worshipful Response	10 to 15	101 WAYS TO WORSHIP—Create a three-dimensional "list" of ways to worship God daily.	Napkins, markers, tape, stepladder

notes:

THE POINT OF "24-HOUR WORSHIP":

You can worship God in everything you do.

THE BIBLE CONNECTION

VARIOUS PASSAGES FROM 1 AND 2 SAMUEL — These passages describe a variety of events in David's life.

VARIOUS PSALMS — David praises God and asks for God's help throughout all of the circumstances of his life.

In this study, kids will create time lines describing what they did the day before the study and then determine whether they worshiped God during the events of that day. They'll also explore how David worshiped God.

By reflecting on David's worshipful responses, kids can discover how to worship God in everything they do as a result of their ongoing interaction with him.

Explore the verses in the "David's Daily Worship" handout (p. 33), then examine the information in the Depthfinder boxes throughout the study to gain a deeper understanding of how these Scriptures connect with your young people.

LEADER TIP for The Study

Whenever groups discuss a list of questions, write the questions on newsprint and tape the newsprint to the wall so groups can discuss the questions at their own pace.

BEFORE THE STUDY

On separate sheets of paper, write the hours of a typical junior higher's day. For example, write "7 a.m." on one sheet of paper, "8 a.m." on another, and continue to "10 p.m." Then tape the sheets of paper in order at even intervals horizontally along one wall of your meeting room.

For the "Encounters With God" activity, write the following list of questions on newsprint, and post the newsprint where everyone can see it.

● What was happening in David's life in the passage from Samuel? How do you think he felt?
● How does the psalm indicate how David worshiped God through his experience?
● How did you respond to the situation on your time line?
● How can you worship God through this type of situation?

24-Hour Worship 27

THE STUDY

LEADER TIP for A Day in the Life

If you're doing this study on a Sunday, you might want to include later hours on the wall, since most junior highers stay up later on weekend nights.

LEADER TIP for A Day in the Life

If you anticipate being tight on time for this study, tape the masking tape lines to the floor before the study. Create one for each student who'll be participating. Then as students arrive, have each one choose a tape line and begin creating his or her time line.

TIME LINE CREATION ▼

A Day in the Life (10 to 15 minutes) As kids arrive, have each of them tape a continuous masking tape line on the floor along the length of your meeting room, parallel to the wall with the sheets of paper you prepared before the study taped to it. Then hand each student a pen.

Say: **Today we're going to explore the topic of worship. Before we delve into the subject, I want you to create a time line of your day yesterday. Use the time line on the wall to guide you. For example, if you talked on the phone with a friend at 3 p.m. yesterday, write that on your masking tape at the spot that lines up with the 3 p.m. sign.**

Allow students five minutes to complete their time lines. Then have each student find a partner next to him or her. Have pairs walk along their time lines, sharing with each other the events of the previous day. When pairs get to the "end of the day," have partners tell each other one positive thing they enjoyed hearing about each other's days, such as a victory in an athletic event or a fun phone call with a friend.

Then say: **Our days are usually full. Whether they're full of school, homework, friends, church gatherings, or watching television, we're almost always occupied.**

But something else is always going on as we're doing these things: our relationship with God. Today we'll explore how you can worship God in everything you do.

Before moving to the next activity, have partners go to a place on either of their time lines when they remember worshiping God. For

---

DEPTH FINDER — UNDERSTANDING THE BIBLE

When we're challenged to follow a Bible character's example of worshiping God, we often say, "Yeah, right. That person was godly, worthy of being in the Bible. I'm just...me." We feel intimidated when we compare ourselves to such people. They seem so holy, so faultless.

But we would do well to remember that these people were merely people. Although David was a king and was called a man after God's own heart, he was human. In fact, some people held him responsible for losses in their own lives, just as we have angered, hurt, or frustrated others in our own lives (see 2 Samuel 16:7-8). And how can anyone forget David's adultery with Bathsheba and his attempt to cover up his sin by murdering her husband?

So when you or your students feel discouraged about your worthiness to praise God, remember David. He was one of us.

24-Hour Worship 28

example, one of them may have sung a praise song while walking to school. When partners have found a spot, have them pray with each other that God will teach them about worship through this study.

INTERACTIVE BIBLE EXPERIENCE ▼

Encounters With God
(25 to 35 minutes)

Say: **You worship God any time you adore and serve him, and according to that definition, you can worship God in everything you do.**

King David in the Bible is a good example of someone who worshiped God in almost every action. In fact, he was called a man after God's own heart. Let's explore some of the events in his life and his worshipful responses to those events.

Give each student a copy of the "David's Daily Worship" handout (p. 33). Choose one type of event from the first column in the handout, and read it aloud. Make sure it's a situation relevant to your kids. Instruct each student to move to a spot on his or her time line that indicates that type of experience. If students didn't have that type of experience the day before the study, have them move to a "default spot" on their time lines, such as the event that happened at 7 p.m. or the experience that most closely resembles the type of experience described.

Then have each student find a partner near him or her, and have partners describe their experiences to each other. Instruct pairs to read the passages from 1 or 2 Samuel and Psalms that correspond to the

---

DEPTH FINDER — UNDERSTANDING KING DAVID

Many of your students may not be familiar with King David. If so, share with your students the following information about David. If you have time, have students read the Bible passages, too.

- David was a shepherd boy, the youngest of eight brothers, who was anointed to become the king of Israel (1 Samuel 16:10-13).
- David served Israel's King Saul and played the harp to comfort him (1 Samuel 16:14-23).
- David confronted and killed Goliath the giant (1 Samuel 17:48-50).
- King Saul became jealous of David's popularity with the Israelites stemming from David's defeat of Goliath (1 Samuel 18:6-9).
- David spent much of his life running from King Saul, who wanted to kill him (1 Samuel 20:30-42).
- After Saul's death, David became king of Israel and Judah (2 Samuel 5:4-5).
- King David was a mighty warrior who conquered many people (2 Samuel 8).
- King David committed adultery with Bathsheba, and when Bathsheba became pregnant with David's child, David arranged to have her husband killed (2 Samuel 11).
- King David's son Absalom attempted to overthrow David, and David had to run for his life (2 Samuel 15).

24-Hour Worship   29

experience they just discussed. After pairs have read the passages, have them discuss the questions posted on the newsprint you prepared before the study.

When students have finished their discussions, take a quick break to play an active game your students enjoy, such as Capture the Flag or Tag. After playing the game for a few minutes, ask:

● **Did you worship God as we played this game? Why or why not?**

● **What are ways we can worship God as we play together?**

● **How can you worship God in a playful situation this week?**

After this discussion, return to the Bible exploration, repeating the process of kids choosing experiences, finding partners, studying the Bible passages, and discussing the questions.

Then serve refreshments. Invite a volunteer to say a prayer of thanks for the food and drinks. As students are eating, ask:

● **Are you worshiping God right now? Why or why not?**

● **How can we worship God as we eat together?**

● **What's one way you can worship God as you enjoy a meal this week?**

If you still have time, continue the Bible exploration. Complete as many sets of experiences and Scriptures as time allows, choosing the experiences most relevant to your group.

When you've finished the Bible study, ask:

● **How do David's worshipful responses to situations encourage you to respond to events in your life?**

● **Did you encounter God through this Bible experience? If so, how?**

● **Did you worship God through our Bible experience? If so, how?**

DEPTH FINDER — UNDERSTANDING WORSHIP

Nicholas Herman's parents raised him to love God, and throughout his adult life, he sought to serve God in everything he did. He began adult life as a soldier, but after being wounded and discharged from the service, he devoted himself to following God. Nicholas Herman joined a monastery where he worked in the kitchen.

By this time, he was known as Brother Lawrence. And today, we know him as the author of *The Practice of the Presence of God*. Through this classic, Brother Lawrence has passed down to us wisdom about incorporating worship into everything we do. Here are just a few of his words of wisdom:

"Is it not much shorter and more direct to do everything for the love of God, to make use of all the labors of one's state in life to show Him that love, and to maintain His presence within us by this communion of our hearts with His? There is no finesse about it; one has only to do it generously and simply."

"Adore Him and praise Him!...The Holy Spirit dwelling in us leads us to love God in a diversity of ways."

"During your meals or during any daily duty, lift your heart up to Him, because even the least little remembrance will please Him. You don't have to pray out loud; He's nearer than you can imagine."

Say: **David is an excellent example for us to follow. He had an ongoing relationship with God and found ways to worship God through almost everything he did. We can do this too. In fact, God would love it if we did!** You can worship God in everything you do.

Right now, worship God for his creation. Turn to the last partner you shared with, and tell that person—who is God's most precious creation—one thing you appreciate about him or her.

WORSHIPFUL RESPONSE ▼

101 Ways to Worship (10 to 15 minutes) Say: **Since you can worship God in everything you do, I challenge you to come up with 101 ways to worship God!**

Set out napkins, tape, and markers. Then have the group brainstorm fun, upbeat ways to worship God daily. For example, kids might suggest writing a song, giving new shoes to a homeless person, sitting still in an empty church sanctuary, stargazing, watching an ant work, humming a praise song while doing math problems, writing a poem of praise for God's help with homework, thanking God for legs with every pedal of a bike ride, or tapping their feet to the rhythm of a favorite Christian song.

LEADER TIP for 101 Ways to Worship

Make sure you have a safe stepladder so that kids can reach the ceiling. If you don't have a stepladder, have kids tape the napkins to a wall.

"I waited patiently for the Lord; he turned to me and heard my cry. He lifted me out of the slimy pit, out of the mud and mire; he set my feet on a rock and gave me a firm place to stand. He put a new song in my mouth, a hymn of praise to our God. Many will see and fear and put their trust in the Lord."

—Psalm 40:1-3

Leader TIP for 101 Ways to Worship

If your students can't brainstorm 101 ideas in the allotted time, leave the supplies in the room, and allow kids to add to the "list" in coming weeks until they come up with 101 ways to worship God.

As students brainstorm, have them all take turns writing the ideas on the napkins, one idea per napkin.

After 101 napkins are filled out, have students work together to tape them to the ceiling. Have students attach tape to one corner of each square and then attach the rest of the tape to the ceiling so the napkin hangs down.

When all of the napkins are taped to the ceiling, say: **You've come up with some great ideas! You can worship God in everything you do, so let's use these ideas to encourage us to worship God in all our actions.**

Have each student choose to do one of the ideas from the list during the week and pull the corresponding napkin from the ceiling to take home. Encourage students to bring their napkins back the next week and report their worship experiences to the class. If you wish, this can be an ongoing challenge as kids exchange napkins or choose new ones from the ceiling.

DAVID'S DAILY WORSHIP

Move to a Spot That Indicates a Time You...	Read a Passage That Describes a Similar Time in King David's Life.	Read a Psalm That Corresponds to That Event.
felt attacked.	1 Samuel 18:10-11—King Saul throws a spear at David.	Psalm 11:1-3, 7—David praises God for his protection and justice.
pretended to be something you aren't.	1 Samuel 21:10–22:1—David pretends to be crazy to escape danger.	Psalm 34:1-7—David praises God for saving his life.
had a disagreement with someone.	1 Samuel 24:11-15—David confronts Saul for pursuing him and trying to kill him.	Psalm 35:22-28—David asks for God's help against unjust people.
felt sad.	1 Samuel 30:3-6; 2 Samuel 1:1-12—David mourns the loss of his people and the deaths of his king and his best friend.	Psalm 40:1-4—David praises God for helping him through difficult times.
fulfilled a responsibility.	2 Samuel 5:3—David is anointed king over Israel.	Psalm 2—David challenges all kings to obey God.
met a challenge and overcame it.	2 Samuel 5:17-25—David conquers the Philistines as God had promised he would.	Psalm 9:1-6—David thanks God for helping him defeat his enemies and praises God as the ruler of the world.
rejoiced in God because of who he is or because of something God did for you.	2 Samuel 6—David brings the Ark of God to Jerusalem and celebrates its arrival.	Psalm 24—David encourages everyone to be pure and praises God for his strength and might.
felt victorious.	2 Samuel 8:3-6—David is victorious over many of his enemies.	Psalm 60:11-12—David asks God's help in battle and proclaims that with God's help his troops can win.
did something wrong.	2 Samuel 12:1-13—The prophet Nathan confronts David about sleeping with another man's wife and murdering that man to cover his own tracks.	Psalm 51:1-2, 10-13—David confesses his sinfulness and asks God to give him a clean, pure heart again.
felt betrayed.	2 Samuel 15:11-14—Many of David's people turn against him, following his son Absalom who wants the kingdom for his own.	Psalm 3:1-6—David praises God for his protection from those who have turned against him.

Permission to photocopy this handout from Group's Core Belief Bible Study Series granted for local church use.
Copyright © Group Publishing, Inc., P.O. Box 481, Loveland, CO 80539.

THE ISSUE: Stress

Stress Reliever

Helping Kids Put Responsibilities in Proper Perspective

by Jim Hawley

■ According to the August/September 1996 issue of Jr. High Ministry Magazine, 68 percent of kids between ten and thirteen years old are afraid they may be physically harmed by bullets. Seventy-three percent are afraid they might be kidnapped. Seventy-one percent of junior high kids are afraid they might contract AIDS. These worries are in addition to the "normal" stresses of junior high, such as grades, dates, sports, and peers.

■ Kids are in desperate need of a safe and quiet place where they can find rest and relief from stress. Worshiping God provides such a place. Worship serves as a reminder to focus on what's important. Worship is a time to let go of our fears as we remember the power of our Creator. Worship gives us an opportunity to give our stress to God and rest in his peace. ■ This study will help your kids understand that worship is not a duty or obligation but a gift that helps us lay down our stress as we focus on and praise almighty God.

> **THE POINT:**
>
> Worship helps you focus on what's important.

The Study
AT A GLANCE

SECTION	MINUTES	WHAT STUDENTS WILL DO	SUPPLIES
Group Experience	10 to 15	**TAKE MY STRESS—PLEASE!**—List stresses on index cards then try to get rid of their stress cards while others put stress cards on them.	Index cards, pens, masking tape
Bible Investigation	15 to 20	**STRESS: THEN AND NOW**—Find examples of stress in Bible characters' lives and explore Romans 12:1-2 as motivation to offer their stress to God.	Bibles, "Stress: Then and Now" handouts (p. 43), pens
Worship Experience	10 to 15	**STRESS SYMBOLS**—Make symbols of the emotions their stress is causing and explore Matthew 6:25-34.	Bibles, newspapers, magazines, paper, envelopes, pens, markers, tape
	10 to 15	**WORSHIP THE STRESS AWAY**—Give their stress symbols to God and rest in his presence while reflecting on Matthew 11:28-30 during a worship experience.	Bible, cassette or CD player, tapes or CDs

notes:

THE POINT OF *"STRESS RELIEVER"*:

Worship helps you focus on what's important.

THE BIBLE CONNECTION

EXODUS 18:13-26; RUTH 1:3-18; NEHEMIAH 4:1-9; 6:1-9; ACTS 15:36-41	These passages describe stressful situations and how various individuals in the Bible dealt with them.
MATTHEW 6:25-34	These verses encourage us not to worry about the physical necessities of life.
MATTHEW 11:28-30	Jesus invites the burdened to find rest in him.
ROMANS 12:1-2	These verses encourage us to worship God through the way we live.

In this study, kids will play a game in which they identify and try to remove stress from their lives while others attempt to add more. Students will explore stressful situations that faced various Bible characters and create symbols of stress they can release to God in a worship experience.

Through this experience, kids will see that stress can be a manageable part of their lives and that entering God's presence in worship is an effective way to handle stress.

Explore the verses in The Bible Connection, then examine the information in the Depthfinder boxes throughout the study to gain a deeper understanding of how these Scriptures connect with your young people.

LEADER TIP for The Study

Because this topic can be so powerful and relevant to kids' lives, your group members may be tempted to get caught up in issues and lose sight of the deeper biblical principle found in The Point. Help your kids grasp The Point by guiding kids to focus on the biblical investigation and discussing how God's truth connects with reality in their lives.

LEADER TIP for The Study

Whenever groups discuss a list of questions, write the questions on newsprint and tape the newsprint to the wall so groups can discuss the questions at their own pace.

THE STUDY

GROUP EXPERIENCE ▼

Take My Stress—Please! (10 to 15 minutes) After all the kids have arrived, give each person three index cards and a pen. Say: **I'd like you to think of three things that stress you out. Write each stress on a separate index card.**

As kids finish their cards, give each student three pieces of masking tape. Have kids help each other tape their own cards to their bodies. When all of the cards have been taped to the students, say: **When I say "go," remove your own stress cards, and stick them on other kids. Keep removing cards as people stick them on you. Ready? Go!**

After a couple of minutes, have kids form groups of four to discuss the following questions:
- **Why are the situations you wrote on the cards stressful to you?**
- **How was removing your stress cards and having cards stuck to you like or unlike the real stress you face?**
- **How does stress make you feel? Explain.**
- **How do you handle stress?**

Ask each group to share its response to one of the questions. Then say: **We all face stress in our lives. Sometimes, as in this activity, stress comes from things that we can't control. Other people and situations often cause stress in our lives. And when the stress becomes unmanageable—as the stress-cards activity did—you can lose sight of what's important. Worship can help us deal with our stress because <u>worship helps you focus on what's important</u>.**

BIBLE INVESTIGATION ▼

Stress: Then and Now (15 to 20 minutes) Have kids form four groups, and have the groups count off from one to four. Give each student a pen and a "Stress: Then and Now" handout (p. 43). Direct each group to study the section on its handout that corresponds with its group number. Instruct all the groups to discuss the questions at the bottom of the handout. After about ten minutes, ask:
- **How could worshiping God have helped the people in the situations you read about?**

Say: **For the next question, brainstorm with your group for three minutes before sharing your responses with the rest of the class.**

Stress Reliever   38

Ask:
● **What are some ways worship can help remove the stress in your life?**

Have each group share its responses with the whole class. Then say: **Worship includes more than just singing songs. You can also worship God through prayer or through the way you live. Worship helps you focus on what's important, and that is why worship is such an effective tool for dealing with stress. In all of the examples your groups read, the leaders dealt with their stress by focusing on God and acting according to God's direction and commands.**

Have a volunteer in each group read Romans 12:1-2 aloud. Then have groups discuss the following questions:
● **What does it mean to "offer our bodies as living sacrifices?"**
● **How can the way we live be a form of worship?**
● **How is being stressed out like being "conformed to the pattern of this world," as described in Romans 12:2?**
● **How can worship renew our minds?**

WORSHIP EXPERIENCE ▼

Stress Symbols (10 to 15 minutes) Ask kids to think silently about this next question:
● **What stressful situation are you facing that you need to give to God?**

Set out newspapers, magazines, paper, envelopes, pens, markers, and tape. Say: **Using these supplies, I want each of you to create a symbol of the emotions you feel that go along with your stressful situation. For example, if your stress makes you feel like your life is out of control, you could create a picture of an automobile accident. The emotional symbol doesn't have to be meaningful to anyone except you.**

After five minutes, have kids form pairs to explain the symbols they've created. Ask:

DEPTH FINDER — **UNDERSTANDING THE STUDY**

Although no detailed information on the actual structure of the early church's worship services is given in the New Testament, several elements of worship can be identified. These include prayer, praise, confession of sin, confession of faith, Scripture reading, preaching, and the celebration of the Lord's Supper.

Contemporary churches include various elements of New Testament worship and have added other elements that are alluded to in records of worship in the early church, such as some form of response time. For the "Worship Experience" portion of this study, elements of praise, prayer, Scripture reading and reflection, and a response time are used to help kids see how worship helps their stressful lives.

Stress Reliever

- What emotions and feelings do you associate with stress?
- What emotions and feelings do you associate with worship?
- What is the most effective way for you to deal with stress?
- How can worship help you give your stress to God?

Give every student a sheet of paper and a pen. Say: **We're going to explore one way to deal with stress. Apply the directions I give you to the situation that you decided you need to give to God. Write your responses on your sheet of paper.** Give kids the following directions:

- Write down everything concerning the problem that is out of your control.
- Write down what you'll do if your plan for dealing with the problem doesn't work.
- Write down everything that could possibly go wrong concerning the problem.
- Write down the worst possible consequences that could result from the problem.

Have kids pair up and discuss the following questions:

- What are some of the problems that your stress could cause?
- How did thinking about those possibilities make you feel?
- How did worrying about the stress in your life help you? Explain.
- Read Matthew 6:25-34. Why do you think Jesus commands us to avoid worrying?

Say: **Jesus tells us not to worry about our needs. Worrying about the stress in your life doesn't help you handle your stress**

"Come to me, all you who are weary and burdened, and I will give you rest. Take my yoke upon you and learn from me, for I am gentle and humble in heart, and you will find rest for your souls. For my yoke is easy and my burden is light."

—Matthew 11:28-30

or overcome it. God has provided a better way for us to handle stress. You're going to have an opportunity to deal with your stress through worship because <u>worship helps you focus on what's important</u>.

Worship the Stress Away (10 to 15 minutes)

Begin the worship experience by having kids move to as private a place as the room allows. Tell kids to worship along with the lyrics or pray about their stress as you play one or two contemporary worship songs. Make the lyrics available to your kids as the songs play. When the songs have ended, ask:
- **How does the message of the songs relate to your own stress?**
- **Does the songs' message help you with your stress? Explain.**
- **How do the songs help you focus on God?**
- **Does focusing on God help you handle your stress? Explain.**

Open a Bible to Matthew 11, and place the open Bible on a table. Say: **This Bible is open to Matthew 11, in which Jesus offers to take our stressful burdens. Jesus encourages you to give your burdens to him. As I read Jesus' words in Matthew 11:28-30, place your stress symbols next to this Bible and silently pray about your stressful situation.**

Read Matthew 11:28-30 aloud, and allow kids to respond and pray. After everyone has had an opportunity to pray, say: <u>**Worship helps you focus on what's important.**</u> **Leave your stress symbol here as a reminder that you have given your stress to God and you will not take the stress back.**

Discard the stress symbols so that kids won't see them again.

> **LEADER TIP for Worship the Stress Away**
>
> Two contemporary songs that illustrate the theme of this study are Rich Mullins' "Hold Me Jesus" from A Liturgy, a Legacy, and a Ragamuffin Band and Jars of Clay's "Flood," from their debut release.

DEPTHFINDER — STRESS AND THE HEALTHY FAMILY

Author Dolores Curran researched families to determine the amount of stress maintained by healthy families. Married men, married women, and single mothers identified the following causes of the most stress in their families:

1. Economics/finances/budgeting
2. Children's behavior/discipline/sibling fighting
3. Insufficient couple time
4. Lack of shared responsibility in the family
5. Communicating with children
6. Insufficient "me" time
7. Guilt for not accomplishing more
8. Spousal relationship (communication, friendship, sex)
9. Insufficient family playtime
10. Overscheduled family calendar

Most of the stressors in this list relate to the children in the family. As kids reach early adolescence, the stress factors for the family increase. Although the stress is significant, those families surveyed were all healthy families that demonstrated strong skills for coping with stress.

Stress Reliever

DEPTHFINDER: UNDERSTANDING STRESS

Psychologists T.H. Holmes and R.H. Rahe developed a stress scale that identifies the impact of stress on health. Each stressful event is assigned a score from 11 to 100, and events are added together to get a cumulative score. A score of 300 indicates a strong probability of a serious illness affecting the stressed person. Although the scale is designed for adults, the impact on teens within highly stressed families is significant. Some of top stressors include:

- 100 Death of spouse
- 73 Divorce
- 65 Marital separation
- 63 Jail detention
- 63 Death of a close family member
- 50 Marriage
- 47 Being fired at work
- 45 Marital reconciliation
- 45 Retirement
- 44 Major change in the health or behavior of a family member
- 40 Pregnancy
- 39 Sexual difficulties
- 39 Gaining a new family member
- 39 Major business readjustment
- 38 Major change in financial state
- 37 Death of a close friend
- 36 Changing to a different line of work
- 35 Major change in number of arguments
- 31 Taking out a loan over $10,000
- 30 Loan or mortgage foreclosure
- 29 Major change in job responsibilities
- 29 Son or daughter leaving home
- 29 In-law troubles
- 28 Outstanding personal achievement
- 26 Wife beginning or ending work outside the home
- 26 Beginning or ending formal schooling
- 25 Major change in living conditions
- 23 Trouble with supervisor
- 20 Change of residence
- 20 Changing to a new school
- 19 Major change in church activities

Totaling the life events for the previous year, the probability of illness in the next two years is as follows:

Less than 150 (low stress)	Low
150-199 (mild stress)	30%
200-299 (moderate stress)	50%
300 or more (major stress)	80%

Stress: Then and Now

Read the descriptions and Scriptures for your assigned person, and discuss the questions listed at the bottom of the page.

1. Moses: Overwhelmed by Overwork

Moses was the leader of the people of Israel. After he led the people out of Egyptian slavery, he led them through the desert for forty years. Moses was the judge over thousands of people. Read Exodus 18:13-26 to see the stress Moses faced.

2. Ruth: Struggling With Relationships

Ruth was a Moabite woman. She married the son of Naomi. Ruth's husband died, and Naomi encouraged Ruth to find another man to marry. Read Ruth 1:3-18 to see how Ruth handled her stress.

3. Nehemiah: Pressure From Enemies

Ancient cities had walls around them to protect them from enemy attacks. Jerusalem's wall had been destroyed earlier, and Nehemiah led workers to rebuild the wall. Read Nehemiah 4:1-9; 6:1-9 to see the stress Nehemiah faced.

4. Paul: Struggling With Relationships

Paul traveled throughout Asia, teaching others about Jesus. He traveled with companions by ship and on foot. One time, Paul was stressed about who he would travel with. Read Acts 15:36-41 to see the stress Paul faced.

Discussion Questions
- What stressful situation was this person facing?
- What did he or she do to handle the stress?
- What do you think of his or her decision? Explain.
- What kind of stress today relates to the situation described in this Bible example?

A New Song, a True Song

by Bob Buller

THE ISSUE: Authenticity

Helping Kids Worship God in Spirit and in Truth

■ Worship is a topic of great interest among churches and youth groups these days. "Traditionalists" often argue that today's praise songs lack the substance and depth of the great hymns of years gone by. Proponents of a more contemporary style of worship, on the other hand, contend that the staid old songs simply aren't relevant to kids today, that we must update our worship services to make them more meaningful to today's younger generation. ■ Arguments for both sides have merit. Both tradition and relevance have a place in Christian worship. Unfortunately, a more important issue seems to have been lost amid the rhetoric of this debate. According to Jesus, the key issue is not the method of worship but the intent behind worship. ■ Jesus taught that true worship is *in spirit* and in *truth*. Authentic worship is the communion of God's Spirit with the spirit of the one worshiping. In addition, genuine worship is true to the character of God in its content and true to the worshiper in its expression. ■ Consequently, worship can be true whether it's

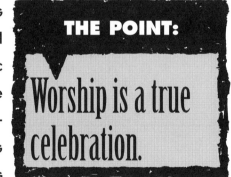

THE POINT:

Worship is a true celebration.

expressed through traditional hymns, contemporary praise songs, symbolic actions, quiet reflection, or verbal declarations of God's greatness. Whenever the *content* of worship is true to who God is and the *expression* of worship is true to the one worshiping, authentic worship—the kind of worship that God desires—is taking place. ■ This study will help your kids move beyond the surface debates about styles of worship to a deeper appreciation of the essence of biblical worship. In so doing, it will free your kids to worship God in new and true ways that honor God and stay true to their own unique personalities.

The Study
AT A GLANCE

SECTION	MINUTES	WHAT STUDENTS WILL DO	SUPPLIES
Opening Experience	5 to 10	AFFIRMATION MANIA—Compete to praise each other's shoes and then discuss how this is like worshiping God without really meaning it.	Bibles, index cards, pencils
Bible Discovery	10 to 15	IDENTIFYING THE ESSENTIALS—Read and discuss John 4:23-24 to learn about true worship, then list biblical reasons to praise God for who he is and what he has done.	Bibles, newsprint, markers, tape
Worship Experience	25 to 30	DISCOVERING THE DIFFERENCES—Learn about different ways to worship God, then lead each other in short worship activities.	Bibles, "Styles of Worship" handouts (pp. 54-55), various worship resources
Closing Application	5 to 10	A TRUE CELEBRATION—Use worship resources to explain how they will worship God during the coming week.	Various worship resources

notes:

THE POINT OF "A NEW SONG, A TRUE SONG":

Worship is a true celebration.

THE BIBLE CONNECTION

PSALMS 103:1-18; 113: 1-9; ROMANS 8:31-39; EPHESIANS 2:13-22 — These passages demonstrate that God is worthy of our worship.

JOHN 4:23-24 — Because God is spirit, God seeks those who worship him in spirit and in truth.

In this study, kids will give and receive meaningless compliments and then discuss how that is like worshiping God without really meaning it. Kids will determine why God is worthy of being worshiped and express worship in an authentic way.

By learning about and experiencing the biblical model of worship, kids will discover that they can worship God in a way that is true to who God is and to who they are. As a result, kids will be encouraged to truly celebrate God and his goodness whenever they worship.

Explore the verses in The Bible Connection, then examine the information in the Depthfinder boxes throughout the study to gain a deeper understanding of how these Scriptures connect with your young people.

BEFORE THE STUDY

For the "Discovering the Differences" and "A True Celebration" activities, gather a wide variety of worship resources, such as praise songbooks, candles, matches, worship tapes, Bibles, kazoos, tambourines, newsprint, markers, and a cross. You'll need one resource for each person.

A New Song, A True Song 47

LEADER TIP for The Study

Because this topic can be so powerful and relevant to kids' lives, your group members may be tempted to get caught up in issues and lose sight of the deeper biblical principle found in The Point. Help your kids grasp The Point by guiding them to focus on the biblical investigation and discussing how God's truth connects with reality in their lives.

LEADER TIP for The Study

Whenever groups discuss a list of questions, write the questions on newsprint and tape the newsprint to the wall so groups can discuss the questions at their own pace.

THE STUDY

OPENING EXPERIENCE ▼

Affirmation Mania (5 to 10 minutes)

After kids arrive, say: **To help each other understand the beauty and wonder of our individuality, I'd like each of you to compliment every person in this room. Reach down to the depths of your soul to find an honest and meaningful compliment that truly expresses the individuality and beauty of each person. Make sure each compliment is unique.**

I almost forgot—all of the compliments must be about the shoes that others are wearing. You can't say what the shoes say about the person, just compliment the shoes. For example, you can say, "Those shoes are very pretty," but you can't say, "Your shoes show that you are a person who knows how to find a good bargain."

Give each person an index card and a pencil. Tell kids they have two minutes to give as many unique compliments as they can. Each time kids praise someone's shoes, they are to have that person initial their cards. But they cannot praise the same person's shoes twice until they have praised everyone else's shoes at least once. Explain that the person who has the most initials at the end of two minutes will receive a prize. Answer any questions, then start the activity.

Give kids a thirty-second warning. When time is up, have kids count the initials they collected. Reward the winner by saying: **I praise you because you're such a complimenting person.**

Have kids form groups of four and discuss the following questions.

DEPTH FINDER — UNDERSTANDING BIBLICAL WORSHIP

Sometimes Christians argue that we should worship God simply for who he is (his character) and not focus on what God has done for us (his actions). Although this notion sounds plausible enough, it is not consistent with the biblical pattern of worship.

Psalm 113, for example, presents a balanced view of how we should worship God by praising God for who he is *and* for what he has done. Verses 4-6, on the one hand, exalt God because he is high above all creation. No one is higher than our God. Verses 7-9, on the other hand, praise God because he stoops down to the needy and raises them to places of prominence. As a whole, the psalm praises God for who he is (the most high) *and* for what he does (stoops down to earth on behalf of his people).

To help your kids understand the connection between God's character and God's actions, have them draw lines on the newsprint from the "Identifying the Essentials" activity, linking the statements of who God is with their corresponding actions.

A New Song, A True Song

After each question, ask for volunteers to report their groups' answers.
- **Did the compliments you received touch your heart? Explain.**
- **Did the compliments you gave reflect your deepest true feelings? Explain.**
- **How well do you remember the compliments you received? the ones you gave?**
- **How are these compliments like the praises we sometimes offer to God? different?**
- **How was the prize like the results of those types of praises?**
- **How do you think God feels when we praise him without meaning it?**
- **Read John 4:23-24. What is God looking for in our worship?**

Say: **Sometimes Christians believe they are worshiping God when they're simply praising him without thinking. But worship is a true celebration. This means that we must truly mean what we say and do when we offer praise to God. So let's spend some time discovering what it means to truly worship God.**

for Affirmation Mania

Junior high kids are especially sensitive to façades. They can easily recognize it when someone is putting on a façade, and they generally view that person with suspicion and cynicism. Remind the kids in your group how little they respect people who put on façades, then inform them that God feels the same way. God wants us to worship him...but only if we do so genuinely.

BIBLE DISCOVERY ▼

Identifying the Essentials (10 to 15 minutes) Have kids remain in their groups. Ask each group to read John 4:23-24 again and discuss the following questions:
- **What does this text say about how we are to worship God?**
- **What do you think it means to worship God in spirit?**
- **What do you think it means to worship God in truth?**

Ask for volunteers to share their groups' insights. Then say: **Worship is a true celebration when it is true to our hearts and true to who God is. To learn more about who God really is, let's see what the Bible says about why we should worship God.**

Give each group a sheet of newsprint and several markers. Assign each group one of the following Bible passages: Psalms 103:1-18; 113:1-9; Romans 8:31-39; and Ephesians 2:13-22. It's OK if several groups have the same Scripture. Instruct groups to write the Scripture reference at the top of their sheets of newsprint and draw two lines to divide the newsprint into three columns. Have groups label the left column of the newsprint "Who God Is," the center column "What God Has Done," and the right column "My Response."

Tell groups to read their passages and to list on the newsprint all the things their passages teach or imply about who God is or what God has done for us. Then have kids write in the third column how they might respond to who God is and what God has done. Encourage groups to involve everyone in the study.

Allow groups five minutes to work, then have them take turns taping their sheets of newsprint to the wall and presenting what they learned to everyone else. If two groups have the same passage, ask one group to present who God is and the other to report what God has done.

When all the groups have reported, ask group members to discuss the following questions. After each question, ask for volunteers to report their groups' answers. Ask:

- **What most impresses you about who God is? what God has done?**
- **How have you seen these qualities and actions in your own life?**
- **How does recognizing who God is and what he has done make you feel?**
- **How might you express these feelings in a true celebration of God?**

Say: **Jesus taught us that those who worship God must do so in spirit and in truth. That means that when we worship God, we should do so in a way that is true and genuine for us and that truly reflects who God is and what he has done in our lives.**

WORSHIP EXPERIENCE ▼

Discovering the Differences (25 to 30 minutes)

Set out the worship resources you gathered before the study.

Say: <u>**Worship is a true celebration**</u> when it comes from our hearts, when it expresses who we really are, and expresses how we feel about God. Of course, since we are all different, there are also different ways to express our praise to God.

> "Yet a time is coming and has now come when the true worshipers will worship the Father in spirit and truth, for they are the kind of worshipers the Father seeks. God is spirit, and his worshipers must worship him in spirit and in truth."
>
> —John 4:23-24

A New Song, A True Song 50

DEPTHFINDER
UNDERSTANDING THE BIBLE

Jesus' conversation with the Samaritan woman in John 4 reveals a great deal about God's perspective on worship. The Samaritan woman believed that where one worshiped was of primary importance. The Samaritans (half-Jews who accepted only the teachings of the first five books of the Old Testament) argued that worship could take place only on Mount Gerizim. However, full Jews who accepted all of the Old Testament as God's Word believed that Jerusalem was the only authorized place of worship. (See 1 Kings 8:1-13.)

Instead of debating the proper place for worship, Jesus shifted the focus away from the physical mechanics of worship to the spiritual dynamics that characterize true worship. The issue is not where one worships but one's attitude in worship. Because God is Spirit, God seeks those who will worship him in spirit and in truth. We worship God "in spirit" when we connect with God—our spirit with God's Spirit—wherever we might be. We worship God "in truth" when the *content* of our worship is true to who God is and the *expression* of our worship is true to who we are. Jesus taught that worship is not so much an act as it is an attitude, the authentic connection of a true worshiper with the one true God.

Have kids form four groups. Give each group one section of the "Styles of Worship" handout (pp. 54-55), making sure that each of the sections has been given to at least one group.

Tell groups they have five minutes to read through their handouts and to plan a three-minute worship activity. The activity should both teach the rest of the group about that style of worship and lead the group in an experience of that style. Instruct kids to involve every member of their groups in the presentations in some way. Encourage kids to make these worship experiences as authentic as possible. Show kids the worship resources you've set out, and invite them to use them as they see fit. Answer any questions, then encourage kids to work quickly to prepare their worship activities.

When there is one minute remaining, instruct kids to finalize their plans. When time is up, invite each group to briefly explain its style of worship and then lead the entire group in its worship activity. Begin with celebrative worship, then proceed to reflective worship, symbolic worship, and declarative worship.

When all the groups have led their activities, have kids re-form their original groups and discuss the following questions. After each question, ask for volunteers to report their groups' answers. Ask:
● **Which of the worship styles did you like most and why?**
● **Which of the worship styles did you like least and why?**
● **Would all the worship styles be a true celebration for you? Why or why not?**
● **Could all the worship styles be a true celebration for others? Why or why not?**
● **How might we benefit by worshiping in all four styles?**

Say: **Because <u>worship is a true celebration</u> of God, it must be true to who God is and to who we are. God created us with different personalities, which means that we can worship

LEADER TIP for Worship Experience

If your church allows it, consider setting out the elements and utensils used to celebrate the Lord's Supper.

God in different ways. The main thing to remember is that whenever we worship God, we should do so in a way that truly expresses who we are and how we feel about the one true God.

CLOSING APPLICATION ▼

Leader Tip for A True Celebration

Do not set out worship items that you must have returned to you as kids may forget, lose, or break them.

A True Celebration (5 to 10 minutes)

Set the worship resources where kids will have access to them. Make sure you have at least one resource for each person.

Say: **Worship is a true celebration** when we authentically express our response to who God is and what he has done in our lives. So let's conclude our time together by deciding how we can do just that.

Ask kids to form new groups based on their preferred styles of worship—those who prefer celebrative worship should group together, those who like reflective worship should group together, and so on. If any worship style is underrepresented, ask for volunteers to move to a new group based on their secondary preference. If any group is larger than five, have it form smaller groups of four or five.

Instruct kids to each think of one reason God is worthy of their worship. Invite kids to select one of the reasons on the newsprint, but

"Praise the LORD, O my soul; all my inmost being, praise his holy name.

"Praise the LORD, O my soul; and forget not all his benefits—who forgives all your sins and heals all your diseases, who redeems your life from the pit and crowns you with love and compassion, who satisfies your desires with good things so that your youth is renewed like the eagle's."

—**Psalm 103:1-5**

A New Song, A True Song

encourage kids to think specifically about how they see this quality and action of God in their lives.

After one minute, have group members share with each other the reasons God is worthy of their worship. Allow several minutes for sharing, and then ask for volunteers to report their groups' reasons to the entire group.

When every group has reported, have kids each choose a worship resource consistent with their preferred worship style and explain to the members of their group how they will use that resource to worship God during the coming week. For example, someone who selected a candle might light a candle every day as a reminder that Jesus is the light of the world, while someone who chose newsprint and a marker might create a "Commitment Poster" to hang in his or her room.

Allow several minutes for group members to share their ideas. Then ask for volunteers to report their groups' worship ideas. After each group has reported, have group members discuss the following questions. After each question, ask for volunteers to report their groups' answers. Ask:

● **What did you like about the worship ideas shared in your group?**
● **What did you like about the ideas described by the other groups?**
● **When does worship not seem to be a true celebration for you?**
● **What can you do to always make worship a true celebration?**

To close, invite group members to pray together, thanking God for being worthy of their worship and committing themselves to follow through with their own worship ideas sometime during the following week. Encourage kids to take their worship resources with them as reminders to worship God during the coming week. Be sure to ask kids to return the items at the next meeting and share with the group how they worshiped God in spirit and in truth.

LEADER TIP for The Study

To help kids remember all that they have learned, challenge them to plan and lead their own worship service that includes all four styles of worship. Encourage kids to choose a particular theme that states who God is and what God has done for them. Help kids think up creative ways to worship God for that theme or truth. Remind kids to incorporate all four worship styles so everyone has the opportunity to experience authentic worship. Schedule a special time for kids to hold and lead the service for the group or the entire church.

A New Song, A True Song

Celebrative

Celebrative worship emphasizes joyful, often musical, expressions of praise. People who prefer this kind of worship feel that they worship God best by praising him in song and movement. Biblical examples of this worship style are found in 2 Samuel 6:14-16; Psalms 92; 96; 98; 149:3; and 150.

Read several of the Scriptures listed above. Then plan a three-minute celebrative worship experience for the rest of the group. For example, you might lead the group in a contemporary praise song, set one of the psalms to a well-known tune, or quickly write your own praise chorus for everyone to sing.

Reflective

Reflective worship focuses on the inner experience of thoughtful contemplation. This worship style makes greater use of silent meditation, readings, and similar types of thought-provoking experiences. People who prefer this worship style feel that they worship God best by meditating about him. In biblical times, meditation was a common way to worship God (Psalms 48:9-10; 77:11-15; 143:5-6; 145:3-5).

Read several of the Scriptures listed above. Then plan a three-minute reflective worship experience for the rest of the group. For example, you might have others close their eyes and think about the words of a Bible passage (maybe Psalm 23 or another passage about God). As you slowly read the words aloud, ask everyone to meditate on attributes of God that you read aloud and explain. Or you could encourage everyone to sit quietly and reflect on what impresses them most about God.

Symbolic

Symbolic worship emphasizes traditional expressions or acts of reverence. People who prefer this kind of worship believe that they worship God best by remembering and re-enacting the key events of their faith. Biblical examples of this worship style include Deuteronomy 16:1-8 and Luke 22:14-20, but many Christians also celebrate key events such as the birth (Advent), death (Good Friday), and resurrection (Easter) of Christ or the coming of the Holy Spirit at Pentecost (Acts 2:1-4).

Read the Scriptures listed above. Then plan a three-minute symbolic worship experience for the rest of the group. For example, you might use candles to explain how Jesus came as God's light to a dark world, have kids secretly write or put their sins on Jesus' cross, or ask group members to create their own symbols to represent one characteristic of God that impresses them.

[Declarative]

Declarative worship focuses on the content of why God should be praised and the commitment to praise him. People who prefer this style of worship believe that they worship God best by learning about him and committing themselves to him. Biblical examples of this worship style include Psalms 111:1-10; 118:1-4; and Ephesians 3:14-21.

Read the Scriptures listed above. Then plan a three-minute declarative praise experience for the rest of the group. For example, you might ask everyone to list reasons God is worthy of worship and then silently commit himself or herself to God. You could read a Bible passage that tells why God should be praised and then ask kids to gather together as a sign of their commitment to praise God. You could encourage kids to think of one praiseworthy thing God has done in their lives and then commit to telling someone else about what God has done.

why Active and Interactive Learning works with teenagers

Let's Start With the Big Picture

Think back to a major life lesson you've learned.
Got it? Now answer these questions:
- Did you learn your lesson from something you read?
- Did you learn it from something you heard?
- Did you learn it from something you experienced?

If you're like 99 percent of your peers, you answered "yes" only to the third question—you learned your life lesson from something you experienced.

This simple test illustrates the most convincing reason for using active and interactive learning with young people: People learn best through experience. Or to put it even more simply, people learn by doing.

Learning by doing is what active learning is all about. No more sitting quietly in chairs and listening to a speaker expound theories about God—that's passive learning. Active learning gets kids out of their chairs and into the experience of life. With active learning, kids get to *do* what they're studying. They *feel* the effects of the principles you teach. They *learn* by experiencing truth firsthand.

Active learning works because it recognizes three basic learning needs and uses them in concert to enable young people to make discoveries on their own and to find practical life applications for the truths they believe.

So what are these three basic learning needs?
1. Teenagers need action.
2. Teenagers need to think.
3. Teenagers need to talk.

Read on to find out exactly how these needs will be met by using the active and interactive learning techniques in Group's Core Belief Bible Study Series in your youth group.

1. Teenagers Need Action

Aircraft pilots know well the difference between passive and active learning. Their passive learning comes through listening to flight instructors and reading flight-instruction books. Their active learning comes through actually flying an airplane or flight simulator. Books and lectures may be helpful, but pilots really learn to fly by manipulating a plane's controls themselves.

We can help young people learn in a similar way. Though we may engage students passively in some reading and listening to teachers, their understanding and application of God's Word will really take off through simulated and real-life experiences.

Forms of active learning include simulation games; role-plays; service projects; experiments; research projects; group pantomimes; mock trials; construction projects; purposeful games; field trips; and, of course, the most powerful form of active learning—real-life experiences.

We can more fully explain active learning by exploring four of its characteristics:

● **Active learning is an adventure.** Passive learning is almost always predictable. Students sit passively while the teacher or speaker follows a planned outline or script.

In active learning, kids may learn lessons the teacher never envisioned. Because the leader trusts students to help create the learning experience, learners may venture into unforeseen discoveries. And often the teacher learns as much as the students.

● **Active learning is fun and captivating.** What are we communicating when we say, "OK, the fun's over—time to talk about God"? What's the hidden message? That joy is separate from God? And that learning is separate from joy?

What a shame.

Active learning is not joyless. One seventh-grader we interviewed clearly remembered her best Sunday school lesson: "Jesus was the light, and we went into a dark room and shut off the lights. We had a candle, and we learned that Jesus is the light and the dark can't shut off the light." That's active learning. Deena enjoyed the lesson. She had fun. And she learned.

Active learning intrigues people. Whether they find a foot-washing experience captivating or maybe a bit uncomfortable, they learn. And they learn on a level deeper than any work sheet or teacher's lecture could ever reach.

● **Active learning involves everyone.** Here the difference between passive and active learning becomes abundantly clear. It's like the difference between watching a football game on television and actually playing in the game.

The "trust walk" provides a good example of involving everyone in active learning. Half of the group members put on blindfolds; the other half serve as guides. The "blind" people trust the guides to lead them through the building or outdoors. The guides prevent the blind people from falling down stairs or tripping over rocks. Everyone needs to participate to learn the inherent lessons of trust, faith, doubt, fear, confidence, and servanthood. Passive spectators of this experience would learn little, but participants learn a great deal.

● **Active learning is focused through debriefing.** Activity simply for activity's sake doesn't usually result in good learning. Debriefing—evaluating an experience by discussing it in pairs or small groups—helps focus the experience and draw out its meaning. Debriefing helps sort and order the information students gather during the experience. It helps learners relate the recently experienced activity to their lives.

The process of debriefing is best started immediately after an experience. We use a three-step process in debriefing: reflection, interpretation, and application.

Reflection—This first step asks the students, "How did you feel?" Active-learning experiences typically evoke an emotional reaction, so it's appropriate to begin debriefing at that level.

Some people ask, "What do feelings have to do with education?" Feelings have everything to do with education. Think back again to that time in your life when you learned a big lesson. In all likelihood, strong feelings accompanied that lesson. Our emotions tend to cement things into our memories.

When you're debriefing, use open-ended questions to probe feelings. Avoid questions that can be answered with a "yes" or "no." Let your learners know that there are no wrong answers to these "feeling" questions. Everyone's feelings are valid.

Interpretation—The next step in the debriefing process asks, "What does this mean to you? How is this experience like or unlike some other aspect of your life?" Now you're asking people to identify a message or principle from the experience.

You want your learners to discover the message for themselves. So instead of telling students your answers, take the time to ask questions that encourage self-discovery. Use Scripture and discussion in pairs or small groups to explore how the actions and effects of the activity might translate to their lives.

Alert! Some of your people may interpret wonderful messages that you never intended. That's not failure! That's the Holy Spirit at work. God allows us to catch different glimpses of his kingdom even when we all look through the same glass.

Application—The final debriefing step asks, "What will you do about it?" This step moves learning into action. Your young people have shared a common experience. They've discovered a principle. Now they must create something new with what they've just experienced and interpreted. They must integrate the message into their lives.

The application stage of debriefing calls for a decision. Ask your students how they'll change, how they'll grow, what they'll do as a result of your time together.

2. Teenagers Need to Think

Today's students have been trained not to think. They aren't dumber than previous generations. We've simply conditioned them not to use their heads.

You see, we've trained our kids to respond with the simplistic answers they think the teacher wants to hear. Fill-in-the-blank student workbooks and teachers who ask dead-end questions such as "What's the capital of Delaware?" have produced kids and adults who have learned not to think.

And it doesn't just happen in junior high or high school. Our children are schooled very early not to think. Teachers attempt to help kids read with nonsensical fill-in-the-blank drills, word scrambles, and missing-letter puzzles.

Helping teenagers think requires a paradigm shift in how we teach. We need to plan for and set aside time for higher-order thinking and be willing to reduce our time spent on lower-order parroting. Group's Core Belief Bible Study Series is designed to help you do just that.

Thinking classrooms look quite different from traditional classrooms. In most church environments, the teacher does most of the talking and hopes that knowledge will transmit from his or her brain to the students'. In thinking settings, the teacher coaches students to ponder, wonder, imagine, and problem-solve.

3. Teenagers Need to Talk

Everyone knows that the person who learns the most in any class is the teacher. Explaining a concept to someone else is usually more helpful to the explainer than to the listener. So why not let the students do more teaching? That's one of the chief benefits of letting kids do the talking. This process is called interactive learning.

What is interactive learning? Interactive learning occurs when students discuss and work cooperatively in pairs or small groups.

Interactive learning encourages learners to work together. It honors the fact that students can learn from one another, not just from the teacher. Students work together in pairs or small groups to accomplish shared goals. They build together, discuss together, and present together. They teach each other and learn from one another. Success as a group is celebrated. Positive interdependence promotes individual and group learning.

Interactive learning not only helps people learn but also helps learners feel better about themselves and get along better with others. It accomplishes these things more effectively than the independent or competitive methods.

Here's a selection of interactive learning techniques that are used in Group's Core Belief Bible Study Series. With any of these models, leaders may assign students to specific partners or small groups. This will maximize cooperation and learning by preventing all the "rowdies" from linking up. And it will allow for new friendships to form outside of established cliques.

Following any period of partner or small-group work, the leader may reconvene the entire class for large-group processing. During this time the teacher may ask for reports or discoveries from individuals or teams. This technique builds in accountability for the teacherless pairs and small groups.

Pair-Share—With this technique each student turns to a partner and responds to a question or problem from the teacher or leader. Every learner responds. There are no passive observers. The teacher may then ask people to share their partners' responses.

Study Partners—Most curricula and most teachers call for Scripture passages to be read to the whole class by one person. One reads; the others doze.

Why not relinquish some teacher control and let partners read and react with each other? They'll all be involved—and will learn more.

Learning Groups—Students work together in small groups to create a model, design artwork, or study a passage or story; then they discuss what they learned through the experience. Each person in the learning group may be assigned a specific role. Here are some examples:

Reader

Recorder (makes notes of key thoughts expressed during the reading or discussion)

Checker (makes sure everyone understands and agrees with answers arrived at by the group)

Encourager (urges silent members to share their thoughts)

When everyone has a specific responsibility, knows what it is, and contributes to a small group, much is accomplished and much is learned.

Summary Partners—One student reads a paragraph, then the partner summarizes the paragraph or interprets its meaning. Partners alternate roles with each paragraph.

The paraphrasing technique also works well in discussions. Anyone who wishes to share a thought must first paraphrase what the previous person said. This sharpens listening skills and demonstrates the power of feedback communication.

Jigsaw—Each person in a small group examines a different concept, Scripture, or part of an issue. Then each teaches the others in the group. Thus, all members teach, and all must learn the others' discoveries. This technique is called a jigsaw because individuals are responsible to their group for different pieces of the puzzle.

JIGSAW EXAMPLE

Here's an example of a jigsaw.

Assign four-person teams. Have teammates each number off from one to four. Have all the Ones go to one corner of the room, all the Twos to another corner, and so on.

Tell team members they're responsible for learning information in their numbered corners and then for teaching their team members when they return to their original teams.

Give the following assignments to various groups:

Ones: Read Psalm 22. Discuss and list the prophecies made about Jesus.

Twos: Read Isaiah 52:13–53:12. Discuss and list the prophecies made about Jesus.

Threes: Read Matthew 27:1-32. Discuss and list the things that happened to Jesus.

Fours: Read Matthew 27:33-66. Discuss and list the things that happened to Jesus.

After the corner groups meet and discuss, instruct all learners to return to their original teams and report what they've learned. Then have each team determine which prophecies about Jesus were fulfilled in the passages from Matthew.

Call on various individuals in each team to report one or two prophecies that were fulfilled.

You Can Do It Too!

All this information may sound revolutionary to you, but it's really not. God has been using active and interactive learning to teach his people for generations. Just look at Abraham and Isaac, Jacob and Esau, Moses and the Israelites, Ruth and Boaz. And then there's Jesus, who used active learning all the time!

Group's Core Belief Bible Study Series makes it easy for you to use active and interactive learning with your group. The active and interactive elements are automatically built in! Just follow the outlines, and watch as your kids grow through experience and positive interaction with others.

> **FOR DEEPER STUDY**
>
> For more information on incorporating active and interactive learning into your work with teenagers, check out these resources:
>
> ● *Why Nobody Learns Much of Anything at Church: And How to Fix It,* by Thom and Joani Schultz (Group Publishing) and
> ● *Do It! Active Learning in Youth Ministry,* by Thom and Joani Schultz (Group Publishing).

your evaluation of  Bible Study Series for junior high/middle school

the truth about WORSHIP

Group Publishing, Inc.
Attention: Core Belief Talk-Back
P.O. Box 481
Loveland, CO 80539
Fax: (970) 669-1994

Please help us continue to provide innovative and useful resources for **ministry**. **After** you've led the studies in this volume, take a moment to fill out this evaluation; then mail or **fax** it to us at the address above. Thanks!

● ● ● ● ● ●

1. As a whole, this book has been (circle one)

not very helpful   very helpful
1   2   3   4   5   6   7   8   9   10

2. The best things about this book:

3. How this book could be improved:

4. What I will change because of this book:

5. Would you be interested in field-testing future Core Belief Bible **Studies and giving us your feed**back? If so, please complete the information below:

Name _____

Street address _____

City _____ State _____ Zip _____

Daytime telephone (___) _____ Date _____

THANKS!

Permission to photocopy this evaluation from Group's Core Belief Bible Study Series **granted for local church use.**
Copyright © Group Publishing, Inc., P.O. Box 481, Loveland, CO 80539.